Unplugged: the Intersection of Technology, Business, and Politics

As I'm writing this book, (2018), Cambridge Analytica outrage is sweeping the United States. Everyone wonders why Mark Zuckerberg saw fit to violate their privacy. In the aftermath, Facebook broke down how they make their money, and Google searches were never the same

Newspayprus (and stuff)

You listen to the radio right? Or watch basic broadcast channels (Fox, ABC,NBC)? The internet Free Services Model (FSM) uses pretty much the same way to make money. You use the service for free , then the company gets paid to place ads on it's service, targeted to *you*. Ever notice that shows usually watched by senior citizens feature commercials for Life Alert? Or that MTV has way too many Proactive commercials? Same thing. On a premium network, such as HBO or Starz or Netflix, there are no commercials because the cost of the content is passed on to *you* , the buyer, or in businesspeople terms, *the consumer*. The model has been around since forever.

When I say forever, I really mean forever. The first ads in recorded human history (at least according to Wikipedia, so basically, it's gotta be true) come from Ancient Egypt. That's right, the pyramids (prolly) had big posters that said "to be reincarnated, please view this papyrus for 30 seconds(with a five second opt-out)". Probably. The point is, as long as there have been capitalists, there had to be advertising.

When the first ton newsletters were invented around the 1800s, the freemium ad model as we know today became the standard. People got a free letter to find out who got married, and found out who was selling three cows and a chicken. The guy with the paper wasn't the customer, the guy who had to sell chickens was the one keeping the newspaper alive.

In the modern era, ads have gotten far more sophisticated. Television and Radio have always chosen to buy ads along the target market, and at the beginning, the Internet did something similar. But eventually, websites and apps began tracking the consumers. Google is making money mostly from targeted info, not just from search . Facebook makes most of its profits from you telling your "friends" about your likes, interests and problems. Ever wonder why if you post "my car just broke down", Google will show results for car dealerships near you? It's not intuition, your computer is listening. If you post on Snapchat that you're headed to the gym Amazon might have recommended protein shakes (*Recommended*

For You!) at the bottom of the page next time you log in. It's not magic, it's just data!

Is it Evil?

Is this data collecting evil? Good question. I'd say no, because capitalism, and they do provide a useful service. Other than the Cambridge Analytica scandal (next chapter) technology that's primarily used for getting your data is usually doing it to provide better service. Heck, Google has had one company motto for a long time. It's three words. Don't Be Evil. Plus, we do sign a Terms and Conditions / Terms of Service, before using the product, so we are giving permission. But that's almost like saying a kid can consent to signing a contract. If we don't know fully what's going on, can we really give permission? I'm sure some of us do, but the majority are not fully aware of what we sign up for. That's not fair. And despite the best of intentions, Cambridge Analytica did happen. It's serious. That's tantamount to (almost like) treason. One thing is for sure, something has to change. We live in a social media influenced world, a social media enhanced world, and quite frankly, I don't even know how to debate anymore without Googling the real answer.

Cambridge Analytica is one of the worst case scenarios on what can happen with data when it's misused. To make a long story short, Cambridge didn't claim the data for legitimate adverts. They bought a program from a guy named Aleksandr Kogan, a so called psychological profile on random people. It used your habits, and the habits of everyone you connected with, to determine the future, as far as your next moves will be. In the digital streets, it's called "Big Data". Benevolently, Big Data is used by places like streaming services to help you shop a little better. If I watch "Breaking Bad" and rate it five stars, next, it'll recommend Mad Men. Harmless right? But in the hands of someone more nefarious, watching "Duck Dynasty" (for example), might lead to the assumption that you'd probably like a 6 month trial of *Gun & Ammo*.

Further, it easily determined who were right wing and who was left wing, who was educated and who was not, who was more easily influenced and who was not. Though the tech was originally created as a sociological evaluation and personality evaluation, it soon became the work of Minority Report and George Orwell's 1984 (good book, I recommend it). And the worst part was that the technology didn't even need to be downloaded by you to get your info! In Australia, it was downloaded by fifty three people, and it winded up getting data for three hundred eleven thousand Australians. In America, Cambridge Analytica took the data from maybe 230 million Facebook users (The United States has around 250 million registered voters, so it's a pretty huge deal) , and they used that precious info to target people maliciously. First I'm gonna break down the two main reasons why it was possible, then we'll get back to that.

Fake News

      Ahh, Fake News. Fake News was probably the most used phrase of the post 2015 political world. Seems like everyone has heard of a fake news story. Nothing is real anymore! we live in a post truth world! Trust nothing! Most "Internet Veterans" have learned how to sort good info from bad years ago, but with smartphones being as ubiquitous as they are, everyone is a journalist and reading about "The News" via Twitter became common. If everyone in the office is saying the same thing, doesn't that make it true? If everyone in the 'hood is saying the same thing, does that make it true? For anyone who's ever been on the receiving end of a particularly vicious piece of hearsay, the answer is a resounding no! Half the time, it's the speaker's way of gaining attention (followers) for themselves, being outrageous for the sake of it, or the weapon of choice in an ongoing conflict. The other half, it's gonna have a grain of truth.

Let's talk about Sarah. Sarah works in an office, she's a proud woman who's beautiful and talented, so she rose quickly in the ranks. "Sarah thinks she's so much better than me! It's probably because she's been dating the boss secretly". Janice in Accounting feels like she should've gotten that promotion, so to her, Sarah is also fat. That will become "The boss got her pregnant!" . Other people have seen her exchanges with the boss and have also considered the interactions flirty. People have also noticed (shrewd detectives that they are) that she's been dressing less revealingly lately. So it's easy to believe. But not to Sarah's husband or her family, or best friends, who know her habits and know that Sarah had her tubes tied a few years ago. Doesn't matter. In 9 months when there's no baby ,the narrative will change to "she must've had him pay to get her an abortion".

People believe what will bring the most entertainment and fulfilment into their lives.

That's a prime example of Fake News. it could possibly be true, it could possibly be explained by various contrivances, and "of course they're gonna deny it!". But today isn't the age of water cooler gossip. Today is the day that "Sarah's Pregnancy" is bigger than just her office, or even her neighborhood. She's on television crying her heart out. Her husband is angrily tweeting denials three times a day. Paparazzi (regular people, probably strangers with a camera phone) are sticking cameras in her father's face asking how he feels about raising a cow (and then he's getting sued for his non-verbal response to said accusation). Whether you think it's sad, or you're condemning her "weak" husband for covering for his adulterous wife, that's the reality we live in. *She obviously should lose her job. How dare she get ahead that way? Don't say it's not true, because if the pregnancy isn't real, *something* happened to cause her to get accused. They're definitely not just coworkers even *if* she didn't abort his baby. If she didn't get pregnant, why hasn't she proven that she didn't take a Plan B?*

Sarah isn't just that poor girl from your office, in the run up to the 2016 elections, Hillary Clinton, Barack Obama, and Donald Trump (Yes, he was one of the first high profile victims of the phenomenon) were all caught in various scandals, the most infamous being Pizzagate. I'm not gonna give that theory any more publicity than is necessary (nor would I encourage you to look it up), but someone took an AR to a pizza joint (not the one that's suspected of being the evil head quarters, mind you, a different one that's a few blocks away) and fired a couple shots. Someone could've been hurt or worse behind Fake News. I don't care who you are or why you did it, violence is always a tragedy, Human life is precious and it needs to be preserved wherever possible.This is serious.

Though I condemn violence, especially this kind, **_STRONGLY_**, no matter the circumstance, the guy who fired those shots believed a horrendous and ghastly criminal conspiracy was going on and the federal executive branch was either paying a blind eye or an active participant. He saw himself as between a rock and a hard place and reacted according to his moral compass. He might've even thought himself a potential hero. But even after he found out how wrong he was, someone else was threatening those poor shop owners three days later, another ardent believer in the conspiracy. So playing "Whack-a-mole" with this issue is incompetent, bordering on criminal negligence. Whether these two guys are foolish, evil, or both is irrelevant, because the next serious Fake News incident might be near you, with a whole new cast of zany characters and guest stars. A serious discussion needs to be had about information, who's getting it, and how to interpret it correctly.

Naivete, Natural Selection, (And stuff)

People are in the horrible habit of trusting sources without verifying. This was a big part of the 2016 presidential election.

Charlamagne Tha God, a hip hop radio jockey, is frequently quoted as saying: "No one cares about the truth when the lie is more entertaining". In these dangerous Digital Streets we so often find ourselves on, we're not being accosted with Salvia, we're being accosted with stories, which are just as dangerous, if not as obvious. And the dealer is not often a shady guy with a greasy look, it's usually a friend, family member, or co worker.

A fish lives underwater, with other fish. Duh. A wolf lives in the forest, with other wolves. Duh. Where does the average liberal live? The average conservative? Amongst their own. People are, generally considered, pack animals. We live, work, hang out, and date within our clique or our tribe or our office or our neighborhood. That means, for the most part, we all lived in our own bubble. That's nothing new. But what's new is everyone having a platform. There are five TV stations, 50 shows, and (at least) 500 Twitter personalities that mirror every type of political leaning, from Marxist to Libertarian to Anarchist. Back in the olden days, even if you thought the media had something to hide, there was at least an "official" story.

That story no longer exists. This is because of the new level of "Media Plurality" we're experiencing today. Take the case of Trayvon Martin, for instance (*buckles seat belt*). One side portrayed him as an innocent child, an avid student who was being courted by Florida A&M University, the other side purported that he was a violent criminal with a history of drug use and possibly in the process of planning a robbery when he was murdered. Which is true? That's the point, we don't know. Both sides have radicalized (made it super loud and dramatic) their message to appeal to what their *customer's* customers (remember, with any free product, *you* are the product) want.

With this new reality where facts are second to what makes the audience feel goo---- actually, I apologize,---- whatever makes the audience feel like they are unequivocally **right**, *and the "opposition" (whoever they may be) is unequivocally* **wrong**, it's easy to understand why we feel so divided. How can we agree on the score when we're watching two different games? If you're watching a football game and your brother announces that the score is 35-30(home team advantage) and your tv says that it's 15-36(away team advantage), how can we talk about the game in peace? After all, the game is right in front of him! He should open his eyes and see that he's being mislead.

Truth is, your brother isn't an idiot. Well, he might be, but this doesn't prove it. He's simply getting his information from a different source. It might sound ludicrous and silly from the perspective of a football game, but in these Digital Streets, we see it all the time. He's not even lying, because he's telling you the score exactly as it was told to him.

This is pretty much what happened in the 2016 presidential election. Both sides were receiving fake news about the opposition. Democrats were sharing the story that Donald Trump had called all Mexicans "murderers and rapists and drug dealers".They said he had called Obama various racial curses in private. They said he did not allow black people on his property. Among other stories. They were enraged, and if it was true, they would have good reason to be. They called him a racist and a fascist and made their people (some of whom, a lot of whom, hadn't even bothered to read the story or watch the video in context) believe that if this man was elected, he would bring a new reign of terror that made the Third Reich look like modern Norway.

Soon it became cool to hate Donald Trump, it became cool to talk badly about his mother, his father, his wives, his children, his businesses, because he was a racist and is less than human (the subject on whether nasty/aggressive/violent anti-fascist activism is ok is a topic for another book. *hint: no it is not*).

Donald Trump supporters were shocked and could do no more then shake their heads and clench their fists because this wasn't the Trump they were voting for. Racist makes people think of Klu Klux Klan hoods and Bull Connors, something out of movies like "Roots" and "Selma", and Donald Trump was the jobs candidate, the equality candidate that was going to create jobs. He was going to destroy affirmative action, the myth of white privilege, and do what other politicians could not. He would Make America Great Again. No way could he be the foaming at the mouth racist the Democrats' supporters said he was. *He's just like us. They don't mean him, they mean us. So we've gotta defend him, and ignore any further*

Hillary Clinton faced similar opposition. They said she didn't believe in Law, unless it suited her. Her alleged crimes range from tax evasion to negligence as Secretary of State to murder, and she gets off scot free. Anyone else commits that many crimes, (s)he's going to jail, do not pass go, do not collect $200. Republican supporters (some of whom, a lot of whom, had not investigated any of the allegations or the resolutions of said allegations) were whipped into a frenzy, and if the charges were proven, might have good reason to be. Many Trump voters believed that Hillary Clinton, if elected , would (after taking all guns) show her flagrant disregard for the law by instituting rash and weak policies that would leave us in a level of poverty that would turn America into a socialist failure that makes Venezuela look like postmodern Japan.

Soon, it became cool to hate Hillary Clinton, it became cool to insult her, her daughter, her husband, her gender, and her virtue. It was okay to do this, because she is a criminal, and a member of the privileged elite, the same elite that had taken so much from regular folks.

When Democrats heard this, they couldn't do anything but shake their heads because this wasn't the Hillary they were voting for. This was an example of American Hope™, a symbol that a woman, through hard work and perseverance, could be anything she wanted to be. So could our daughters. Wasn't that what conservatives claim to believe in? They couldn't attack her skills, so they attack her character. Isn't it just like those deplorable people to be sexist? Maybe they just can't handle that a black man and then a woman would become president. They're racist. No way she could commit any type of crime. *She's our hopes and dreams. So we've gotta defend her, and ignore any further accusations, because the people accusing him never had any credibility, they don't care about facts.*

Do those two realities sound familiar? Did you hear yourself on either paragraph? If so, maybe we should take a question if we've been hoodwinked. No matter who you're in favor of, Fake News about both parties was spread. That information meant that many voters were not getting enough true facts to make an educated decision about who should lead The United States of America. That's not fair. In any situation, people should be judged by what they've done, and what they can do, not exaggerations, half truths, or hearsay.

Russia and stuff

Okay, let's go back to tech. Cookies. Phishing. Big Data. Etc. I'll break down those words in a second. In 2015, Russians sought a way to influence the American election, based on targeted information. Their targets were those most susceptible to exaggeration, half truths, and hearsays. How did they do this? Through Phishing, Cookies, and Big Data.

The technology to turn a "digital footprint" into a "digital profile" has existed for a while. Most of this is done through what're called Cookies. Cookies are placed on websites to record what you do there and who you are. Remember the "Recommended for You" section of Amazon? Cookies is how that's done. It shows who you are, where you are, and your browsing habits.

Let's use your Google search history for example. If you've Googled "Fox News" "Guns & Ammo" and "All Lives Matter", stands to reason that that person is a Conservative. If you've Googled "MSNBC" "420" and "free college" , you're probably a liberal. At least, that's what Google thinks. And that's what their customers think

Phishing is a little bit more sneaky. It's usually when someone sends you an email that says "your (service here) account is being hacked, to reset your account, click this link"(No,that's not a real link). The link they'd send you is usually an invite to enter your password and username (or worst case scenario, your Social Security Number), which is then put into some hacker's list of emails/SSNs. He or she can then go through it whenever they want, and you usually won't be able to tell until it's too late. Phishing is what happened to John Podesta, the Hillary Clinton campaign chairman. This is what got this whole situation started.

The common belief is that Russians hacked our election to undermine our belief in democracy. After all, if Democracy can be influenced by a few people behind computers, what good is it? It was most likely a heavy moral loss to many Americans who truly believe that the most beautiful part of our country is the right to choose our leaders. After all, if we can't choose our leaders, how are we any better than an aristocracy? Tampering with our elections turns us from a government of the people into a plutocracy(government for the rich, by the rich), an aristocracy (a government ruled by royalty and elites, to work in their favor), or worse, another Russian colony. Most people, all things considered, don't want their sovereignty threatened.

How'd they do it, you might ask? That's the crazy part. Once they managed to use Phishing to get enough sensitive American data to create believable hearsays, they crafted somewhat believable stories about both Hillary Clinton and Donald Trump.

Once they had the stories, they selected which people to send which stories to (it would be foolish to send, for example, a story about Hillary Clinton smoking marijuana to the average Colorado Democrat). They selected people by purchasing their Cookie information from places like Facebook, and turning those Cookies into personality profiles. Remember my "MSNBC" "420" and "free college" Google user from a few pages ago? Russians saw information like that and concluded if this is the type of person to send an Anti Hillary article to or an Anti Trump one. Once the message is sent, it doesn't have to be sent to too many other people, because of word of mouth. Nine times out of ten, if your mother, best friend, and favorite cousin are all telling you the same thing, it really doesn't matter who else has a different perspective or why, the first information you got is probably good enough for you.

So how do we stay safe in these Digital Streets? Well first, let's talk about combating fake news. the first step is education. No, not always going back to school, sometimes it's just taking a brief course or reading a book (like this one, thank you for getting this far). Learn logic and fact checking. When you read the news, watch for "could've" "possibly" and "allegedly" , those words can mean there's no facts to back it up. Expand your "media diet". Liberals too. Whenever you see a story or a tweet, before you believe it, look for an opposing news source and analyze both stories. Whatever is in both is most likely true. For example, a *Huffington Post* reader might want to check Breitbart to separate fact from bias (what they're trying to sell you), and vice versa. If the entire news story ends with "to protect yourself, buy our product" it's probably a half truth at best. Emails that have been forward a half dozen times also are probably half true, as are Social Network messages from strangers with only a link.

For Phishing, be very careful. That's the golden rule for everything tech related, but especially with Phishing. Double check who sent you the link before typing any info you wouldn't put on your Facebook wall. That usually means passwords, social security numbers, and credit card numbers. But other stuff can be dangerous too.Try to get in the habit of using "https" when visiting a site instead of "http". Like https://mail.Google.com instead of http://mail.Google.com . I recommend being very observant (almost paranoid) whenever some website (or a Facebook quiz) asks for your birthday, your Mother's maiden name, pet names, your address, or where you went to school, stuff like that. Any of those sound familiar? Those are usually security questions. Someone can take that information and use it to get access to your important stuff like your email inbox, your bank login, or your credit score stuff. If you're getting emails from companies you've never heard of or only heard of once, or getting emails asking for money or inviting you to meet Hot Local Women in your area, don't click the link, just unsubscribe. Whenever you're creating an account with a non-business internet service (like that site you watch movies on), use the company's name for your middle name/last name, that way, if they sell your data, you know who did it. If you write their customer service department and let them know you're not pleased, you'll probably get free stuff. Just a thought ;).

Cookies are pretty much everywhere on the web, and I can't exactly say don't use websites that have Cookies, but if you take good precautions against fake news and Phishing, most Cookies won't be harmful. If you insist on trying to cut down the amount of Cookies on a site, go to your browser (Firefox, Internet Explorer, Chrome,etc) and look for the Settings menu. Once you've found Settings, there should be a button to press for Do-Not-Track, and one for "Block Third Party Cookies". Click both. Now you're pretty protected. Use Private Browsing, usually "Ctrl+Shift+N" on most browsers, and try to remember to sign out and close the site whenever you're done with something.

The Business of Politics

Politics is a messy business. Who hasn't heard that before?
My favorite definition of politics is a Merriam Webster one that says:
"the total complex of relations between people living in society". It's
a good one because many people define politics solely as the realm
of politicians, when in fact "politics", in a few words, is the art of

getting things done by a group. One part of the group, or even a single member, may want one thing, another part of the group or single member may want the opposite, and the third member of the group wants to put the whole operation to rest and build a crab shack. So there are more voices than reasonable plans of action. Goes without saying right? So people make their voices louder through the extra noise by combining (In political speak that's called a Lobby or a party , with the two biggest Parties being Democrats and Republicans). That Part or Lobby will make themselves even louder with the help of political action committees (PACs). high-rollers retain the services of a "SuperPAC" to donate unlimited amounts. So money is a big part of politics. Is it a big deal? Well,political finance reform has been necessary since the days of Rome, but how do you suggest people get their message out? It's not enough to dislike the way things are done, positive change only comes when there's a better system to replace the old one.

        But in the meantime, SuperPACs are a thing. Big businesses like the NRA, Comcast, etc. make a point of being heavy donors because there can be no them (at least, no effective them), without pro-gun and anti net neutrality (Google it) politicians. Planned Parenthood, GLAAD, and yes, Marijuana advocates also have their own lobbies and expensive (Super)PACs that want to push their agendas forward. Business and Politics, at this time, work very closely together. This might not be all for ill. Businesses are job creators and surveyors of mood in America, so they do give politicians a perspective on what the man on the ground needs. Might not always be the best perspective, but a perspective.

In the short term, if you want to make your voices heard to politicians, you've got to vote. And lobby. Google your representative/Senators/mayor/alderman/councilperson to get their information, and then call/write/show up at the office to make your voice heard. Be willing to listen too.

Maybe take a page out of their book and start your own PAC! Especially if you've got means (most people have, if not both, either an hour a week or ten dollars a week they could spend on something important). I hear people talking about criminal justice reform and yelling "free Such N Such" "free So N So" but little movement among those with the right to vote to elect or campaign for the judges, Governors (the President can only pardon fed cases), and prosecutors (prosecutors have maybe 50% of the power in a criminal case, Defense lawyers have 15%, judges have 15%, the defendant and jury split the remaining 20%, more or less) that are sympathetic to criminal justice reform. That's just one example. In every community, the people most dissatisfied with the power being thrown around by government folks and business folks have a voice that matters. That is, if you use it in the right places and times, with the right message.

The Politics of Business

Most big businesses are publicly traded. Somewhere around half of the Fortune 500 is public. Public companies tend to appoint CEOs based on results. Maybe it was the Recession, maybe it's technology and people wanting things instantly, or just the way things are done nowadays, but either way, there's not much room for dropping profits in the modern boardroom. As a CEO, in addition to the already strenuous task of being responsible for the jobs of everyone in the company (sometimes more than 2 million people, in Wal-Mart's case), a CEO also has to please shareholders, some of whom don't understand the company, the market or
just plain don't think long term.

Life Rule: Not thinking long term is the second quickest way to mess up a good thing.

When you buy a piece of the company, called stock ("investing"), you're basically loaning the company money, under the agreement that your money will be paid back, and with interest. The shareholders (people who bought the little pieces of the company) are the ones that actually own the company. The CEO is usually an employee too! Look at the example of Steve Jobs (the iPod/ Apple guy). Even though he was a co-founder,and came up with the ideas behind Apple, he had someone to answer to. Same thing with Jack Dorsey, founder of Twitter. Stockholders are skittish, so often it's in a CEO's best interest to make quick money above all else, because not doing that is the quickest way to get fired.

Life Rule: Before getting upset that someone "isn't doing their job", ask yourself "Will they get fired for not doing xyz?" Not should they be fired, will they be fired. If the answer is no, then whatever request you have is secondary at best.

Don't believe this? Follow stocks. Follow the companies of stocks you pick, the behavior of their CEOs, and the pattern between the two. Stocks go low? The CEO is going to be stressed. CEO does something good? Stocks go up. They're connected. If you'd like a company to do something different, the best thing to do is buy stocks and pay attention to owner's meetings. Can't afford stock yet? Try out options. Options, some of them going for as low as 10, 20, or fifty dollars, are a slightly less risky way to learn how the market moves. Still, watch how the little changes between CEOs and stocks work. In the future, once you've got money, be an advocate for responsible growth as a shareholder.

The Technology of Business

B2B . Ever heard the phrase? Business to Business sales make up a sizeable portion of most companies. After all, a business tends to be less wishy-washy than a single customer. A single person has a million different needs, but a business has only one: *How can I get stuff done better than I did yesterday?* Remember the "free service model" I talked about? Another business is usually the customer. Google makes pretty much all of it's "search" money doing business to business transactions. Long story short, B2B is definitely a great field to consider for anyone with experience working in a company environment (Fast Food, Office Work, Retail, Corporate, etc.) just notice what the company is missing and try to find out how you can fill that need.

If you think about it, anyone working can be considered a B2B, at least philosophically.
Let's look at entertainment for example. Sean Carter is one of the greatest rappers ever. False. Sean Carter is the man behind the brand/company known as "Jay-Z". Jay-Z not only makes rap music from scratch, but markets said raps in appealing ways, with a great return on investment. Jay-Z also has since diversified into production, a record label, touring, advertising, real estate, etc. Plenty of companies would like to do a B2B transaction with Jay-Z, and by extension, the brand/company's CEO, Sean Carter.

Difference between him and most people? *He's not a businessman, he's a business,man.*

Even when I'm punching the clock, Ayinde (me) is not "an employee", I'm the CEO of "Ayinde K. Williams" a brand/company with a list of services, and I rent some of them out on a set schedule with another company. While there, I'm making my business, which is my "brand", better by sharpening or diversifying my skills. Whether that skill is software engineering, flipping burgers, writing this book, working a register, or filing paperwork, I'm honing the "brand" of Ayinde K. Williams, and hopefully raising my "company's" stock, with the end goal of moving my company the way I want it to move. Everything I do is not only on me, it's on the "Ayinde K. Williams" brand. I'm the CEO of that, so I work night and day to ask the same question every business asks: *How can I get stuff done better than I did yesterday?*

The Politics of Technology

Aaaand we're back to lobbying. One of the biggest issues today is Green Energy. It's a major engine of change, but are also a perfect model of how and why lobbies are so useful to big business.

Green Energy is "the wave" nowadays. It's trendy, and a lot of people see it as necessary. Electric cars, solar power, smart buildings, hydrogen, anything that doesn't make the air stink. This is a pretty tricky situation, because just like the typewriter vs laptops and horses vs cars, cheap green tech can put a lot of people out of business. Coal, oil, and Natural Gas are a strong, well-paying source of employment for a lot of people. We live in a democracy, so you've got to expect people to represent and protect their own interests

Life Tip: *I love cartoons and comic books, but life is neither. Villains and Monsters, people who do wrong for wrong's sake, are very rare, so rare that even most lawyers and social workers have only met a handful. Mostly, it's just that your current opponent's*

So, Big Energy (Coal, Oil, & Gas), has lobbied very hard to make sure they can get anti climate change candidates into office, and once they're in office, they want pro climate bills defeated quickly, preferably quietly. Lobbying is two fold though. Most political strategists will tell you that if you want to get people passionate, the cheapest way (useful to win a campaign, but not long term) is to not just get something for people to go for, but something against. So there's got to be just as much white noise that makes the opponent unequivocally **wrong** as there is campaigning that positions the anti climate change group as unequivocally **right**.

Whether Climate Change is real or a hoax, green energy is cheaper for the consumer in the long run, so it's coming, whether those companies like it or not. But what catches the eye about the whole snafu is that it's a very basic example of how the whole lobbying thing works.

a. A controversial development happens in the world.(the development of, for example, cheap electric engines)
b. It's great news for the people in position to take advantage. (physicists and engineers who have the skills and means to make electric vehicles)
c. It's bad news for the people who have developed an opposite skill set. (People who work in Coal, Oil, & Gas)
d. Both are going to want the government to make their lives easier
e. Both will wrap their profit in a social issue (cheap energy, oil dependency, & climate change for Green Tech. Jobs, Faith in God, and the humble nobility of the common man for Big Energy) .
f. They find a group in the country that cares about that specific issue, and fund a battle via proxy (go-betweens and stand-ins), with a combination of proving themselves right and proving the enemy wrong.
g. The battle continues for... a while.

Does this all seem like a waste of time? The main problem isn't even the disagreement, it's that a serious debate has become more like a football rivalry than a political issue, it's more about us vs them than getting results. How many Climate Change supporters can buy a Tesla? How many deniers actually work for a coal mine? If green tech is the future like people say, it's not supposed to be for just the Coastal Elites. Let's place some new resources in the same areas that are getting hit by the loss of Coal, Oil, and Gas jobs, and build them to hire people that are actually losing their jobs, not just transplants from the West Coast that'll only gentrify the area. Undercut the support, and be a legit better option, no amount of oil money will make that lobby attractive to a smart person.

The Business of Technology

      Technology isn't what it used to be. The late 90s and Early 2000s was what is now called "The dot com boom". You could make money just by adding ".com" to the end of your business's already established name. That's not a joke. It was a time of innovation and greed and chaos and magic and terrible taste. Every new website was definitely not Yahoo or AOL, a potential hundred million to billion dollar idea. Most of them were elaborate scams that were focused on getting people excited about the idea, not actually turning a profit. "Interest" , not the financial kind where you got paid for getting a loan, "interest" like how many people are into your new idea, was considered a serious form of capital that was as valuable, if not more, than having something people have already bought.

      That all came crashing down in the early 2000s (with a brief comeback during the iOS "App Store" craze & the Bitcoin/Blockchain craze) , but even when there's not a current craze, there's a certain divide in technology. A quarter of the industry is traditional, either coming from another sector, or having been burned hard in one of the last three crazes; they want solid numbers only, quick profits, a get-in, get-out investment strategy. The other extreme is the quarter that is ready to ride the wave of whatever next craze is, hopefully at the right moment. Most people are in the middle, and that's where the best decisions are made

The best type of investment is a combination of on paper and good judgement. For example, Is it a wise move to invest in a "headphones" company in 2018 that doesn't want to diversify into wireless? No, unless they're making collector's items (like the record player companies) .Even if the numbers are so far fantastic, because that market is getting smaller, it's unwise to pursue that long term.

Life Rule: When making a decision with serious repercussions, don't think about "what should happen next" or "what's happening now". You've got to use both, because sometimes "what should happen" is based on an outdated theory, and sometimes "what's happening" has some factors you don't know about, so it could possibly be unsustainable. Wisdom is in balance and the Middle Way

The Technology of Politics (The Editorial)

Do you care about your privacy? Of course you do. I guess the question is, how much? Privacy has been an issue and will continue to be an issue as technology develops. I wanted to use this last chapter to speak on what it means. I want to answer the question "Why should I care about privacy if I have nothing to hide?"

Well, I'd first start with a simple comparison "Why should I care about free speech if I have nothing important to say?" Think on that, and think about an environment where people have to lie. There are very few fates in the first world (provided your needs for food, clothing, and safety are met) that are worse than living in a situation where you've got to lie day in and day out. It eats at the spirit. Atheists, am I right? No matter your religious preference, lying every day isn't fun. Privacy stops that. Privacy gives you the freedom to be *you*, after a hard day of work. Not the sanitized version that you present to others, I mean the real you. The one with strong opinions. The one whose hobbies might not be "everyone's business". The real you. We need Internet privacy for the same reason you'd like a shower curtain or blinds on your windows. Think on that

Well, my mom always said "when you know better you do better", so now's the opportunity to do it. Thanks for listening, signing off!

About the Author

Ayinde K. Williams is a student of life, web developer, artist, and Minister. He wrote *Unplugged: the Intersection of Tech, Business, and Politics* with the goal of reaching those who might find stuff like this boring.